CW00321423

Bradley Trevor Greive's two previous books, *The Blue Day Book* and *Dear Mum*, are both international bestsellers. *The Blue Day Book* was also the bestselling Australian book of the year *2000*. In addition to writing his inspiring, funny books, BTG is an artist, cartoonist, furniture and toy designer, animation director, screen-writer, and ex-paratroop platoon leader. He lives in Sydney, Australia.

Other books by Bradley Trevor Greive

The Blue Day Book
Dear Mum

Looking for Mr. Right

BRADLEY TREVOR GREIVE

RANDOM HOUSE AUSTRALIA

Random House Australia Pty Ltd
20 Alfred Street, Milsons Point, NSW 2061
http://www.randomhouse.com.au

Sydney   New York   Toronto
London   Auckland   Johannesburg

First published by Andrews McMeel Publishing, Kansas City, Missouri, in 2001
This Random House Australia edition first published in 2001

Copyright © Bradley Trevor Greive, 2001

All rights reserved. No part of this publication may be reproduced, stored in a retrieval system, or
transmitted in any form or by any means, electronic, mechanical, photocopying, recording or otherwise, without the prior written permission of the publisher.

National Library of Australia
Cataloguing-in-Publication Entry

Greive, Bradley Trevor.
Looking for Mr Right.

ISBN 1 74051 063 1.

1. Mate selection - Humour. 2. Man-woman relationships -
Humour. I. Title.

177.6
Book design by Holly Camerlinck
Printed by Tien Wah Press (PTE) Limited in Singapore
10 9 8 7 6 5 4 3 2 1

ACKNOWLEDGMENTS

This little book represents yet another joyful collaboration with Christine Schillig and the Andrews McMeel family. I would also like to thank Jane Palfreyman at Random House (Australia) for her support and friendship and award an overdue commendation to my tireless foot soldier, Anita Arnold.

I shudder to think why there are so many amusing photographs of men looking extremely foolish. Nevertheless, I am extremely grateful to the talented photographers who have fossilized these male foibles, and I am indebted to the wonderful people who helped me unearth them, namely Norma Scott, Bronwyn Stewart, Adrian Seaforth, Andrew Stephenson, Karl Mellington, Anne Sidlo, and Simone Cater.

As always, I reserve the last word for Mr. Albert J. Zuckerman of Writers House in New York. Al is not just my agent, he is my hero.

Not only because he once slapped Chairman Mao's face after sneaking into a Beijing Communist party rally in 1958 disguised as a circus bear or because he has consistently said *no* to hard drugs at White House fund-raisers since the '70s. Al is my hero because he fearlessly puts body and soul on the line for his authors every day of his life.

Hail Zuckerman. We who are about to write salute you!

Looking for Mr. Right

*I*t turns out that men are just as frustrating now as they were when you first became aware of their existence.

Men are ridiculously pig-headed and stubborn.

They are completely unable to express their feelings,   3

4 because men have no idea what real strength is.

Men are obsessed with size and appearance.

6   They are inherently jealous and suspicious,

often paranoid about relationships,

8   and will go to great lengths to avoid commitment.

And you know all those childish pet habits they had that
you thought they would eventually grow out of?

Well, they don't.

Basically, they are unreliable and goofy,

because the fact is, men are not very bright.

It's no wonder, then, that trying to have a quality
relationship with a man can be the best way
to bring on a migraine.

Of course, it's easy to ignore the downside and
all the warning signs when an exciting new romance
is just starting.

At this stage, you not only accept his pointless interests,
you embrace them as "cute" and "quirky".

You may even try to involve yourself in his silly games
to maximize "quality time" together.

You'll do everything you possibly can to maintain
the relationship's momentum.

So you can't hear, or won't listen to, that little voice inside your head whispering "Danger, danger, danger! Loser alert! Loser alert!"

You don't trust your female intuition that something
unpleasant is about to happen.

19

Instead, you put all your feelings, hopes, and dreams into his hands, becoming a complete romantic martyr.

And then, all of a sudden, you come crashing down to earth
in the most dramatic fashion imaginable.

Aaaaaaaaaaaaaaaargh!
Another nightmare relationship!

"D'oh!"
You can't believe it's happened again.

Meanwhile, [insert the name of a girl you hated in high school] is flaunting more "ice" than Alaska

and seems well on her way to having a
dream family with perfect teeth and no body odour.
Can you imagine her life?

"Wow, Mummy, that turkey sure looks like
George Hamilton. Mmmmm!"

No thanks.

All in all you're left feeling like you've been
soaking in a bathtub full of squid livers.
Men, yeee-uck! Who needs them?

But is dedicating yourself to a chaste life of religious
devotion, high fibre granola and sensible underwear
the only way for a modern woman to find true bliss?

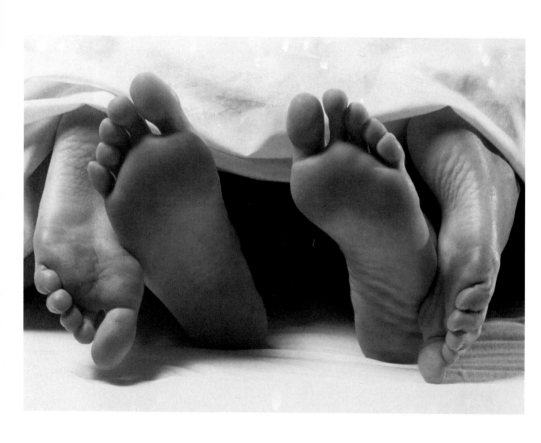

No, it probably isn't.

In your heart you know how life is supposed to turn out.
We've all seen how Mother Nature brings two creatures
together in the right place at the right time. 31

32   They then fall madly in love and live happily ever after.

And so you ask yourself: "If a penguin can have a worthwhile, stimulating relationship, why the hell can't I?" 33

Or maybe you ask yourself:

"Would I be happier if I started dating a penguin?"

This might sound like a stupid question until you wake up
and realize that men and women do not always form
the natural union you've been led to believe. 35

And thus, in some cases a woman needs a man like a bear
36   needs a bicycle (or is it "like a fish needs a snowmobile"?).

Anyway, the point is that men and women are
essentially different species, which is why it can be so hard
for them to stay together. 37

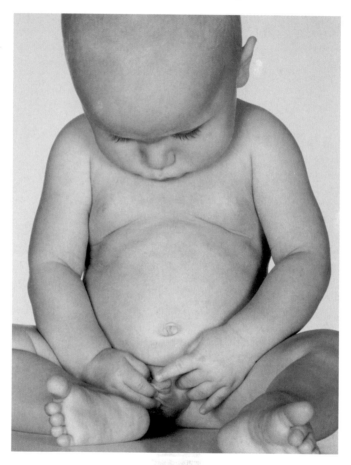

Right from birth there is a small but crucial difference
between men and women that becomes more obvious
and intrusive later in life.

(No, it's not that. If it were, a simple modification
would solve all your problems.)

39

It's that men have a reduced mental capacity that warps their perception of reality and ability to reason. They have a terribly deluded sense of self-importance, which makes it very difficult for them to interact with more intelligent life-forms.

In layman's terms, as a species, men are simply not
as evolved as women. 41

This is obviously the cause of the painfully backward male
attitude toward relationships, which I'm pleased to say has
gradually been refined over the last million years,

although there is still substantial room for improvement. 43

What men desperately need are good male role models.
Sadly, there are none.

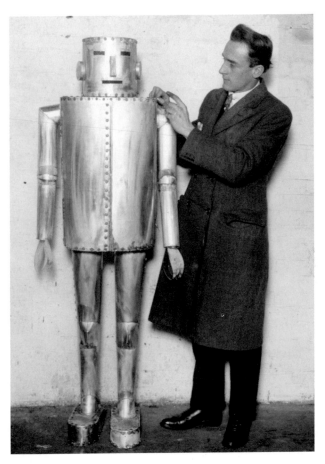

Even if we could build a "perfect man" from scratch,
he would still have flaws. You must embrace this fact
if you wish to stay sane.

(Believe me, some of our greatest minds have gone mad
in their vain attempts to eradicate male flaws.)

In terms of strange behaviour, it doesn't get much
more bizarre than when a man attempts to secure a
woman's romantic interest.

Men have a perversely simple sexual agenda that can best be described as an overwhelming blend of vanity and urgency.

48

"Hey, look at me."

"Look at me!"

"Look at meeeeeee!!!"

It's not uncommon for a young woman with low self-esteem
to find this superficial display both intoxicating and
compelling. Without thinking, she dives right in to
the fray with an equally superficial response.

She begins to fret about her appearance rather than focus on her many outstanding qualities as an intelligent human being.

53

"Will he think I'm sexy enough?"

"Will he find me wholesome enough?"

"Is he allergic to feathers?"

Such concerns are demeaning and detract from what really makes a woman attractive—confidence, intelligence, charisma, purpose, dignity, and a relaxed sense of self.

When such important principles are overlooked, a woman will try far too hard to impress her date, which can only create unrealistic expectations for future outings and be injurious to her health and reputation.

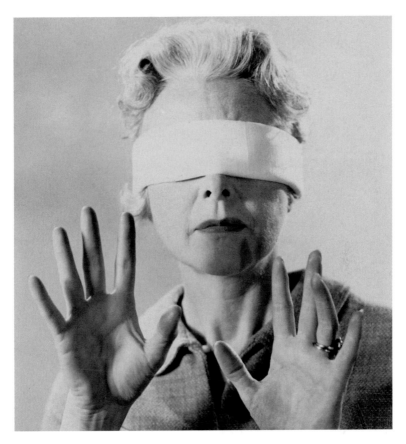

One of the keys to a successful relationship is knowing what
you're looking for—you might not have room in your life
for a man right now. But even if you don't know what you
want, you should acknowledge that and go on from there. 59

(Men don't know what they want either, but they
don't even know that they don't know. This is clearly
not a good platform to build a relationship on.)

When you are evaluating a potential "Mr. Right" candidate, the only important questions are about how you feel. Do you feel special? Do you feel loved and respected? Do you feel that the relationship is bringing out your best?

Too often women get bogged down on incidental issues,
like "What is his mother like?"

"How would we look going out together?" and

64 "How many relationships has he been in?"

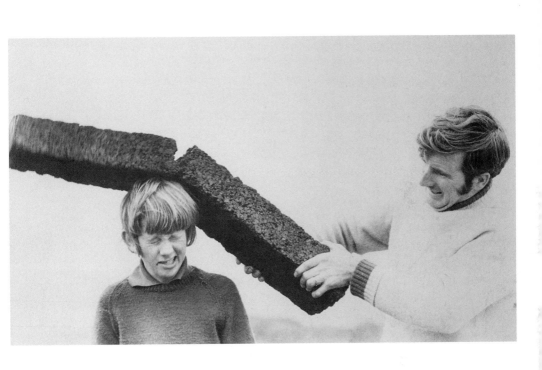

Wondering about such abstruse hypotheticals as
"What kind of father would he be?"

and "How might he look in fifty years?" are really
just a form of self-inflicted mental abuse.

So forget about the past or the distant future. There is
no way to reveal your destiny other than to make it
turn out the way you want it to.

Anyway, no one can really see into the future, and anyone
who says they can is not someone whom you would like
to be stuck next to on a long international flight.

Of course, women who focus on style over substance
eventually find what they want: a devilishly
handsome man who is oh-so-smooth and sophisticated,

is built like an ancient god,

and is not afraid to cry during old movies.

In short, an absolute angel.

There's just one itsy-bitsy problem. . . .

And if you think finding out that Santa Claus
is really just a fat old man with a hairy bottom and
a fake beard was a horrific surprise,

just wait till you come home to find your boyfriend
trying on your underwear with his "squash buddy".

75

This merely serves to remind us once again how important
it is to listen to that little voice inside your head when
it says "MR. WRONG!"

It's way too late when he starts that old
"it's not you, it's me" waffle,

or you accidentally stumble across some unusual snapshots from his overseas "business trip".

As a side note, if your man is unfaithful you can always
hire a professional thug to rearrange his features, 79

80   and, for an additional fee, jam a walking stick up his butt.

Of course, there is only one known cure for infidelity.

Seriously, though, if a man doesn't measure up
you should take immediate action.

You only have one life to live, and the clock is ticking.

You can't afford to answer the door for every creep
who comes knocking,

you don't have time to chase men
who aren't worth catching,

86   and you certainly shouldn't be fighting over them.

You should leave that sort of unseemly and childish display
to men, who have nothing better to do.

But no matter what happens in your relationships,
you must never forget that falling down and getting
back up again is a part of life.

Even more importantly, you must never forget that
only you are responsible for your happiness.
No other person is necessary to complete you.

Think back to the times when you were truly happy—
to when you felt you could do or be anything you wanted.
Well, nothing has changed.

The world is still the same wonderful place it was
when you were a little girl.

The only difference is now you are old enough, smart enough, confident enough, and strong enough to take on any challenge that life wants to throw at you and to realize your dreams on *your* terms.

There has never been a better time to be a woman
in the history of the planet than right now.
You can do whatever you want.

Women are smashing through age-old barriers in every
conceivable facet of life.

They are having more fun making and breaking rules than ever before. And what's more, scientific studies show that kicking male chauvinist butt actually reduces cellulite!

Whether it's qualifications, adventure, career, men,
or money, you can have as much as you want.

Hey, if you can visualize it—

you can have it!

So why wait helplessly for the fate train to run you over?

Start your engines ladies, the world is yours.

Heed the spirit of those who went before you:
"Attack, attack, attack!"

Get out there and take what's yours.

Here's the bottom line. If you are true to yourself and can love yourself for who you are, then other people will love you for who you are too and will treat you accordingly. 103

And by pursuing your dreams with passion,
you will attract a man who is pursuing his dreams
with passion—an enlightened, inspired man
who will appreciate the real you.

When you run into this lucky individual, you'll know
it was meant to be.

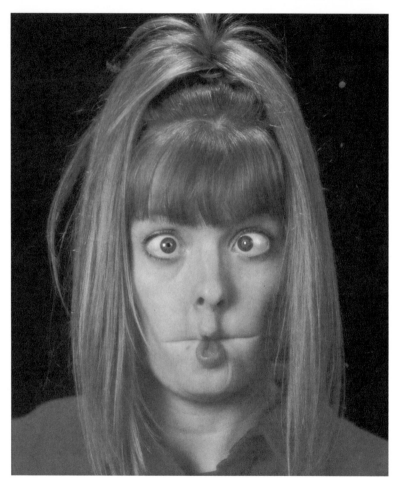

(Hint: If you kiss him and it feels like your lips have
been molested by a giant lemon, he ain't the one.)

The sound of Mr. Right's voice will make you feel
dizzy with desire.

You'll go weak at the knees when you see him.
(And so will he.)

In his eyes you will always be glamorous and beautiful.

He will be someone you can grow old with
(gracefully or otherwise).

Someone who will show you exactly how true love
is meant to feel.

This is not a summer fantasy; this is reality.
And what's more, you deserve it!

Not because you're the most graceful butterfly
in the garden,   113

but simply because you're you, and you're
pretty damn fabulous!

At the end of the day, it's your party.

Enjoy it.